From the Heart to the Homeland

*A Collection of Poems by
Brad Solomon*

Copyright © 2025

All Rights Reserved.

Dedicated to Harrie W – thank you for your unending support during this terrible war. You helped so much during these dark times and your encouragement to write and express my pain this way is why this book was created. These poems are written in memory of all those who fell in Israel on 7 October 2023 and for the memories of those who gave their lives to protect the land that I love. May their memories be a blessing. Thank you to my therapist Harrie. I appreciate you.

About the Author

Brad Solomon

Brad Solomon is a proud Zionist who spent much of 2024 volunteering in Israel in the aftermath of the October 7 massacres and the ensuing war with Hamas. Throughout his time in Israel, he channelled his emotions into poetry, using writing as a cathartic release for the pain and devastation he witnessed.

A dedicated advocate for Israel, Brad is committed to supporting those affected by the war. Proceeds from this book will go toward Shanti Farm Rescue, an animal shelter in northern Israel, and Sword of Iron, a volunteer group and non-profit organization.

Brad also adopted a dog from Israel, a survivor of the war who lost her family in its early days. When not writing or advocating, he runs The CTG Group, an executive coaching company.

Table of Contents

About the Author i
And Yet I Carry On 1
From the Heart to the Homeland 3
Tikva, what is Hope? 5
A Home, A Promise 7
Melody of Home 8
With Courage and Trust 9
Light a Candle 10
Home at Last 11
Fire in My Soul 13
Those Who Give Without Asking 14
And Still I Hope 16
In the Stillness 18
Israel, My Heart 20
Hope Lives Eternal 22
Proud Jew 23
A Nation's Heart 24
A Yellow Ribbon 25
Whispering Colours 26
Hurt Settles Deep 27
The Shanti Farm 28
Shuva Ahim 30

Hope Beneath the Fire 32
The Soldier's Promise 34
The Swords of Iron... 35
A Homeland's Cry 37
F*ck HAMAS 39
Restless Dreams.. 40
A Soldier... 42
We Will Dance Again 44
The Heartbeat of My Homeland............................. 47
To Protect Us 49
Hope Is a Flame 51
Hope Again.. 53
In the trembling sky 54
We Fight 55
Bring Them Home 58
Blue and White 60
Yet Still, We Rise 61

And Yet I Carry On

I feel lost, I feel empty, the echoes of sorrow, vast and unending.

Sadness brews, then gives way to rage, a fire unfurling, trapped in a cage.

I feel low, I feel hollow,

a drifting soul with only one path to follow.

And yet-I carry on.

I feel seen, I feel heard, though every word seems swallowed by hurt.

The war continues, it rages on, as rockets rain, as missiles spawn.

Lives are shattered, torn apart, and hope slips from a weary heart.

Yet still-I carry on.

I try my hardest not to cry, but tears linger, close by.

My heart aches in endless sway, my soul yearns for peace, far away.

I see the hate in countless eyes, and every question meets the skies-

Why, why, why?

But silence answers with a sigh.

And still-I carry on.

Though my being aches, my spirit worn,
Though grief and rage leave me torn,
Though hope falters like a fading dawn,
I gather strength, and carry on
Am Yisrael Chai

From the Heart to the Homeland

From the heart to the homeland, a pulse beats strong,
A rhythm of history, an unbroken song.
The **blue and white flag** waves in the sky,
A symbol of promise that will never die.

It **rises from the ashes like a phoenix from the flames**,
Through trials and sorrow, through loss and names.

Yet still, it soars, defying the night,
Fueled by a fire of **hope and light, hope and light**.

There's **grit and resilience on everyone's face**,
Etched in their footsteps, their battles, their grace.
Through **pain and sorrow, grief and sadness**,
They forge ahead, refusing the madness.

For **the heart is strong, the soldiers are stronger**,
But **the people are stronger still**, lasting longer.
As if the energy of all who stand,
Flows **from the heart to the homeland**.

And through it all, a truth remains,
A song unshaken by time or chains.
One voice, one people, steadfast and high—
Am Yisrael Chai.

Tikva, what is Hope?

What is hope?
A whisper in the storm,
A flame that flickers yet keeps us warm.
It is the voice that calls our name,
The dream that burns despite the pain.

What hope there is—
In the lion's roar in Israel's air,
In flags that dance with defiant care.
Hearts scream loudly, unafraid,
A symphony of courage, serenade.

Where is hope?
Is it lost in shadow, hidden by fear?
Does it linger in the places once held dear?
Or is it in the hands that reach, the eyes that see,
The soil, the sky, the land that must be free?

What does hope look like?
A child's first step, a rising sun,
The march of many, bound as one.
A light that pierces, a banner high,
A star that anchors the restless sky.

What does hope feel like?
A heartbeat strong, a lifeline near,
The taste of joy that dissolves the tears.
It's the mighty roar, the echoing call,
The strength to rise when we might fall.

Where has hope gone?
Has it faded, has it died?
Why does it hide, where does it reside?
Bring me hope—call it by name,
Summon the spark, reignite the flame.

For hope does die last.
And before it goes, its mighty light
Shines so bright it consumes the night.
It burns, it blinds, it carves a way,
For hope is tomorrow in the face of today.

Or is hope just a word?
A fleeting sound, a hollow cry,
A fragile wing that cannot fly?
Is hope just a feeling, soft and surreal,
Or is it the anchor, the only real?

Is hope even real?
Or is hope my Tikva, my guiding star,
The song of my soul, the who we are.
In roaring lions, in hearts that scream,
Hope is the promise, the unyielding dream.

A Home, A Promise

Oh my beloved Israel, steadfast and true,
A land of courage, of skies so blue.
Hostages in my thoughts, their silent screams,
Their freedom a prayer in restless dreams.

Volunteers giving, selflessly they stand,
With open hearts and tireless hands.
They heal the wounds, rebuild what's torn,
Through endless nights and weary morns.

Shattered families, a pain so vast,
Lives divided, futures recast.
Shattered dreams, like fragile glass,
Still, burning hope refuses to pass.

Muted smiles carry the weight of loss,
A silent tribute to the heavy cost.
Yet even in sorrow, a spark remains,
A will unbroken, despite the pain.

Israel in my heart, a beacon of light,
Guiding us forward through the night.
Through tears and struggle, it will endure,
A home, a promise—unshaken, pure.

Melody of Home

In the quiet of evening,
Pain lingers like smoke,
Suffering wraps around our hearts,
A heavy cloak we can't shed.

Time slips through trembling hands,
Each moment marked by loss,
Hurt echoes in silence,
The weight of uncried tears.

Guilt stirs in laughter,
An unwelcome guest at the table,
As shadows dance where joy once lived,
No music to lighten the air.

Yet, in the stillness,
Love remains a fragile thread, binding hope to the hollow,
Waiting, always waiting, for their return,
For the melody of home.

With Courage and Trust

My heart aches as the sky is on fire,
Resilient and brave, we rise from the pyre.
Hate can't win, though the world stands by,
Love and peace must triumph, though many deny.

Israel is a lion, a sword of iron bright,
The world screams ceasefire when we defend our right.
It doesn't seem fair, it doesn't seem just,
But stand tall we must, with courage and trust.

Though silent when we are attacked, they demand our troops cease,
Yet Israel stands tall, a pillar of peace.
Through every storm, through every fight,
We will be here, defending our light.

Light a Candle

Light a candle with hope in your heart,
It never gets light until it's been dark.
Where are you? What are you feeling?
We are all with you; can you feel us sending you healing?

The sunsets feel empty while you are away,
The days stretch long, and the nights don't sway.
Sleep is something I used to do,
I wonder if you sleep at all, too.

Light a candle for hope, light a candle for peace,
The soul of the nation longs for release.
fill the air, let love find its way— Come home, come home, let us feel your hearts today.

Home at Last

They look so thin, they look so tired,

Ghosts of themselves, yet unbroken, inspired.

A nation holds its breath so tight,

As shadows return to the warmth of light.

Their families hold them, fierce, afraid

For the first time in months and months, they've stayed.

Tears, smiles, exhaustion blend,

The torment bends but does not end.

Yellow ribbons are not needed here,

Their return is etched in love, not mere

Symbols hung on trees in wait.

They are home, though bruised by fate.

Ignored by the world at large, left unseen,
But not by those whose prayers have been
A steady drum, a whispered name,
A beacon in the darkened frame.

Tonight, they sleep in their own beds,
Resting weary hearts and heads.
And though the road is rough and long,
Tonight, we breathe. Tonight, they're home.

Fire in My Soul

Fire in my belly, fire in my soul,
A blaze untamed, a burning goal.
Fire in my head, fire to be told,
A story fierce, a heart so bold.

Fires everywhere, fires down below,
Fires in the heart, in the silent snow.
Fires in the sky, fires in the sea,
Fires in the villages, fires to be free.

Fires in my eyes, fires in my toes,
Fires in the memories only I know.
Fires every day, fires in the night,
Fires bring me warmth, fires bring me light.

Fires in the ashes, fires set me free,
Fires in the life that burns within me.

Those Who Give Without Asking

Volunteers arrive,

From all corners of belief,

With hands open, hearts steady,

And a quiet fire of purpose.

No banners to wave,

Only the weight of service,

Carried lightly,

Shared in laughter and sweat.

Packing meals,

Lifting harvests,

Kneading hope into the soil.

Small acts,

Woven together,

Build bridges of friendship,

Rebuild the land.

Israel rises anew,

Touched by the hands

Of those who give

Without asking.

And Still I Hope

Each week passes, and still I hope,

A flicker in the darkness,

No sign of life,

No sign of life.

Where could you be,

What can you see,

As days blend into nights,

The world continues,

Yet I stand still,

Holding on to whispers.

Each week passes, and still I hope,

Are you cold,

Are you scared,

Do you feel my heart calling,

Echoing your name into the void,

A prayer woven in the air.

I will not stop calling your name,

Screaming it from the rooftops,

Clinging to hope that you can hear me,

Soul to soul,

And one day, you will be home,

Back where you belong,

Where love awaits,

Unbroken, unwavering.

Each week passes, and still I hope,

I call,

For light where shadows linger,

For answers that elude the silence,

For the warmth of your embrace,

Until the stars guide you back.

In the Stillness

In the quiet of evening,

Pain lingers like smoke,

Suffering wraps around our hearts,

A heavy cloak we can't shed.

Time slips through trembling hands,

Each moment marked by loss,

Hurt echoes in silence,

The weight of uncried tears.

Guilt stirs in laughter,

An unwelcome guest at the table,

As shadows dance where joy once lived,

No music to lighten the air.

Yet, in the stillness,

Love remains a fragile thread,

Binding hope to the hollow,

Waiting, always waiting,

For their return,

For the melody of home.

Israel, My Heart

Beneath the blue and white so pure,

The Star of David stands secure.

Proud and strong, enchanting sight,

A beacon shining through the night.

Not all will grasp, not all will see,

The soul that yearns for harmony.

Yet peace demands a careful thread,

Not a loss of self, nor spirit bled.

When the world misreads your truth,

When the moon deceives in silver sleuth,

Still in my blood, you boldly flow,

Israel, my heart, my steady glow.

Ever giving, ever bright,

Your courage guides us through the fight.

For in your pride and love, we see,

The strength of home, eternity.

Hope Lives Eternal

Swords of iron, lions roar,

Soldiers weary, battle sore.

Families torn, hearts in grief,

A nation suffers, seeks relief.

PTSD in every face,

The echoes linger, time won't erase.

How do we fight? How do we stand,

With trembling hearts and empty hands?

No more tears, they've all been shed,

For those we've lost, for words unsaid.

Yet hope lives eternal, a flame in the sky,

And the flag keeps flying, proud and high.

Proud Jew

Relief in the chaos, grief all around,
Lost souls searching, no peace to be found.
Yet hope flickers gently, a soft, steady flame,
Volunteers offer solace, no need for acclaim.

Can we smile through the pain, the lies in the air?
Tell me, why do they lie? Why isn't it fair?
But I stand in the truth, unshaken, upright,
I feel what is right, like the dawn after night.

I am proud, I am strong, my soul knows what's true,
I am a Jew—yes, a proud Jew.
With Israel in my heart, a love burning bright,
My beacon, my heritage, **my guiding light.**

A Nation's Heart

A nation hurts, a nation cries,
Pain reflected in weary eyes.
Families broken, dreams undone,
Grief beneath a fading sun.

Help rises from within our land,
For who will heal, if not our hand?
When others turn, when eyes grow blind,
We keep our hearts and souls aligned.

We serve, we give, we share the weight,
We offer compassion in the face of fate.
Yet still, it feels a hollow shore—
So much to give, I wish I could do more.

A Yellow Ribbon

A yellow ribbon, soft and bright,
A symbol of hope through endless night.
A yellow ribbon, tied with care,
A symbol of waiting, a silent prayer.

A yellow ribbon, desire's flame,
A longing voice, a whispered name.
A yellow ribbon, clenched so tight,
A symbol of courage, a symbol of fight.

Tears and dreams, worry and pain,
Hope persists, though hearts are strained.
Devastation, the weight unknown,
A yellow ribbon pleads: bring them home.

Whispering Colours

Dark skies stretch endlessly, heavy with the weight of a thousand unshed tears. Rockets still coming, their fiery arcs piercing the fragile silence,
Yet our spirits refuse to break.
Hostages still hidden from us, their names whispered in prayers that rise like smoke,
Carried by winds that know no borders.

But we have hope, the unyielding thread that binds us to tomorrow.
We have the IDF, standing steadfast as the guardian of our dreams, a shield against the chaos.
We have love, fierce and unrelenting, a fire that warms even the coldest of nights.
We have each other, hands clasped tightly, hearts beating as one, a rhythm that no storm can silence.

And we have belief, the quiet certainty that these dark skies will eventually lighten.
The dawn will come, painting the world anew,
Its colours whispering that even in the longest night,
Light never truly disappears.

Hurt Settles Deep

In shadows of pain,

Suffering wraps its cold arms.

Time running out,

A relentless tide.

Hurt settles deep,

Tears carve our faces,

Guilt for laughing,

Each joy feels stolen.

No more music,

No more fun,

Until they are home,

Until love conquers loss.

The Shanti Farm

Dust swirls gently through the air,

Life, once broken, finds repair.

Dogs bark loudly all day long,

A chorus of the lost, a weary song.

Cats prowl soft, the cows stand near,

Goats and pigs with eyes of fear.

Rabbits hop, and turkeys cry,

Birds of all shapes take to the sky.

The noise, the noise—it wears them thin,

But the silent voices lie within.

Hurt and alone, left to despair,

Until an angel found them there.

An earth angel, with locks of gold,

A Rasta heart, both fierce and bold.

Giving help to the voiceless, love to the weak,

Restoring dignity, the hope they seek.

The Shanti whispers, forever a part,

A home for the voiceless, etched in my heart.

In the dust, the noise, the love they pour,

The Shanti is in my soul evermore.

Shuva Ahim

Shuva Junction, a sacred place,
A soldier's refuge, a warm embrace.
Away from the battle, the heat, the strife,
A moment of normal, a taste of life.

Weary and hungry, they gather here,
Food all day, comfort near.
Three brothers stand, their light shines through,
Turning darkness to hope, old to new.

Where death once reigned, destruction fell,
Now rises a haven, a tale to tell.
Three thousand meals, day and night,
Clothes and medicines, easing the fight.

Massage, healing, guitars that sing,

Volunteers bring joy, the simplest things.

Songs of hope, strength untied,

Am Yisrael Chai, we sing with pride.

Shuva Junction, where hearts ignite,

A beacon of love in Israel's fight.

Hope Beneath the Fire

Rockets soar, fire burns bright,

Shells and drones pierce the night.

The sky lights up in a deadly show,

But the Iron Dome stands, a shield below.

Flags wave high on apartment walls,

Life persists as the darkness calls.

The streets hum loud, the beaches stay full,

A people unbroken, their hearts still whole.

Children sing with voices clear,

While adults weep, their grief sincere.

The war drags on, a heavy weight,

Everyone weary, yet refusing hate.

Hope doesn't fade, it burns inside,

For our brothers and sisters who cannot hide.

In terror tunnels, they endure the strife,

As we cling to the promise of peace and life.

The Soldier's Promise

A soldier stands in uniform proud,

With fire in their heart, their head unbowed.

Tired and weary, yet holding their ground,

In the echoes of battle, courage resounds.

A gun by their side, a shield of steel,

They march through the storm, their resolve is real.

Brave and stoic, yet their smile remains,

Heroic through struggle, through losses and pain.

They fight for Israel, for a nation's light,

Protecting the land with all their might.

Without question, they answer the call,

Their hope lifts a people, their strength guides us all.

Am Yisrael Chai, forever we sing,

For the soldiers who guard our freedom's wing.

The Swords of Iron

Hate, hate, hate—

All they give me is hate.

Why do they hate?

Why do they lie?

Why is the truth left to wither and die?

Too many questions, too many whys—

I'm tired of the lies,

Tired of the stupidity,

Tired of the poison of antisemitism's cry.

But hope still flickers, sharp and bright.

It whispers: *Hold on—this isn't the night.*

The swords of iron gleam in the sun,

And with them, the fight for justice is won.

Israel must win, and Israel will stand,

A shield for the people, a torch in their hand.

Not just for themselves, but for us all—

For those who resist the shadows' call.

My heart fights with them,

My soul burns too,

For truth, for peace,

For a world made new.

Let this hatred crumble, let the lies decay,

Let swords of iron carve a brighter day.

Israel fights not just for their land,

But for freedom's light to forever expand.

A Homeland's Cry

Blue and white ripple against the azure sky, the Star of David gleaming as flags catch the wind, whispering stories of resilience.
Beneath their shadows, the golden sands of Israel's beaches meet the Mediterranean's gentle waves, where the sunsets paint the heavens in hues of orange and pink.
The beauty is so vivid it aches, a fragile contrast to the heart-wrenching sadness that lingers like a shadow across the land.

Hope weaves through everyone's dreams, a thread of light binding a nation scarred yet unbroken.
But even hope feels fragile when you think of the suffering.
Hostages wait in the darkness, their cries muted by walls, hidden behind the terror tunnels that snake below, carrying fear where peace should bloom.

Every reel I watch, every post I read—each image, each word—reminds me of the pain my beautiful homeland endures.
It's a collage of heartbreak: a mother clutching her child, a soldier standing steadfast under a tattered flag, a prayer whispered in trembling hands.

And yet, even in the sadness, there's something indomitable.
The blue and white still fly.
The Star of David still shines.
The sunsets still burn brilliant, as if to remind us that even the longest nights will end.

This is my homeland. Beautiful, broken, resilient.
And in every wave, every gust of wind, every tear shed and every prayer offered, I feel its heartbeat—steady and strong, calling us all to hope, to dream, to fight for the brighter dawn we know must come.

F*ck HAMAS

Do you hate more than you love?

Is death the only thing you're thinking of?

Do you feel weak, so you destroy,

Turning killing into your twisted joy?

Does your hatred mask your fear,

A void that's always drawing near?

Do you hate yourself as much as us?

Your lies crumble, your violence disgusts.

Hamas are terrorists, wake up and see,

No justice lives in their cruelty.

It's time to rise, the world must amass,

And say it loud: **Fuck Hamas.**

Restless Dreams

Oh my beloved Israel, steadfast and true,

A land of courage, of skies so blue.

Hostages in my thoughts, their silence screams,

Their freedom a prayer in restless dreams.

Volunteers giving, selflessly they stand,

With open hearts and tireless hands.

They heal the wounds, rebuild what's torn,

Through endless nights and weary morns.

Shattered families, a pain so vast,

Lives divided, futures recast.

Shattered dreams, like fragile glass,

Still, burning hope refuses to pass.

Muted smiles carry the weight of loss,

A silent tribute to the heavy cost.

Yet even in sorrow, a spark remains,

A will unbroken, despite the pain.

Israel in my heart, a beacon of light,

Guiding us forward through the night.

Through tears and struggle, it will endure,

A home, a promise—unshaken, pure.

A Soldier

A soldier stands, their gun by their side,

A quiet figure where courage and fear collide.

Friendships forged in fire's glow,

Strength that only trials know.

Their commitment, a solemn vow,

To protect the land they plow.

Their heroism, unsung, unseen,

Yet woven into every scene.

Love for homeland, a sacred flame,

Love for family, the heart's true aim.

Bravery carved in moments dire,

Courage ignited by inner fire.

Protection held like a shield of light,

Fear a shadow in the night.

Knowledge honed through bitter strife,

Strength to bear the weight of life.

In the IDF, they stand as one,

Beneath the burning desert sun.

Desire to see the world made whole,

Truth a beacon, their guiding goal.

A soldier stands, steadfast and true,

A quiet hero, through and through.

We Will Dance Again

Tzeva Adom

6:29 a.m.

Rockets tear the sky.

Sirens wail their warning cry.

Guns bark their fatal song—

We just came to dance.

Music,

Friends,

Love's embrace,

Happiness in every face.

Tents and touch,

Massage, crystals, dreams.

Drugs to float,

To forget what it means

To live in a fractured world.

We just came to dance.

Running.

Screaming.

Screaming.

Running.

Left, right—where to go?

Shadows take form.

Terrorists, everywhere.

Bullets rain,

Each sound a shattering prayer.

Running.

Screams pierce the morning air.

Then—

Silence.

Total silence.

The quiet breath of death,

Destruction, horror,

Hopes extinguished

In an instant.

But—

We will dance again.

Through fire,

Through grief,

Through ash and pain,

We will reclaim

The music,

The friends,

The love,

The light.

We will rise to the beat of our hearts,

And we will dance again.

The Heartbeat of My Homeland

Blue and white dance in the sky,

The Star of David shining high.

Flags in the wind, a steadfast song,

A call to a people brave and strong.

On golden sands where waves embrace,

Sunsets bleed beauty across this place.

Yet heart-wrenching sadness shadows the land,

Hope clings tightly, hand in hand.

Hostages suffer in the dark below,

Terror tunnels where shadows grow.

Dreams are pierced, yet still they gleam,

A flicker of light in a fragile dream.

Every reel I watch, every post I read,

Tells of my homeland's aching need.

Mothers weep, soldiers stand tall,

Prayers rise where tears may fall.

Still, blue and white refuse to fade,

The Star of David, unafraid.

And sunsets burn with endless might,

A promise of day after the night.

This is my homeland, broken yet whole,

Its heartbeat echoes in my soul.

Through every tear, through every cry,

Israel endures—its spirit won't die.

To Protect Us

Run towards danger,

Stand on the front line.

No fear ahead,

No one left behind.

For Israel, for the world,

You bear the fight.

Your gift is your courage,

Your unwavering might.

Without question,

With honour you strive,

Giving all of yourself

So others survive.

To protect us,

You rise with the dawn,

A shield in the darkness,

A hope to lean on.

Through fire and chaos,

Through shadows and pain,

Your sacrifice echoes—

A hero's refrain.

For Israel, for the world,

You hold the light,

Guarding the future

With all of your might.

Hope Is a Flame

Beneath the sky so vast and wide,

The world spins gently, side by side.

Each day a canvas, fresh and bright,

Painted in hues of dark and light.

The wind whispers secrets to the trees,

The moon dances on the evening breeze.

Stars flicker softly, dreams take flight,

In the quiet embrace of the night.

Through every moment, small and grand,

Life unfolds in shifting sand.

With every breath, a story told,

In the pages of the heart, so bold.

Hope is a flame that softly glows,

Guiding us where the river flows.

Through joy and sorrow, we remain,

Bound by love, and free from pain.

Amidst the desert, proud and grand,

A blue and white flag waves through the sand.

The Star of David shines so bright,

A symbol of strength, a beacon of light.

In the breeze, it flutters high,

A testament beneath the sky.

Israel's heart beats strong and true,

A land reborn, a dream anew.

Hope Again

Sand whispers,
Sea sighs,
Shells scatter,
Pebbles rest.

Light flickers,
Darkness stirs.

Hope rises,
Hate lingers.
A dance of shadows,
A battle of breath.

Hope stands,
Light endures.

Israel awakens.
The lion roars,
Swords of iron clash,
A spark ignites—hope again.

In the trembling sky

Sunset bleeds into the horizon,
Drones hum faintly in the distance,
Sirens, sirens—a nightly alarm,
Too loud to ignore.

I hear them in my sleep,
Waiting to be woken,
My dreams laced with
Iron domes,
Protection stretched thin
Over Israel's heart.

Find me hope
In the trembling sky,
In the quiet after chaos,
In the flag that still flies high.

We Fight

We fight,

Swords of iron glinting beneath a blood-red sky,

The clash of metal rising like a lion's roar.

We strive,

Through fire and ash,

Each step etched into the earth with purpose.

We hope,

A fragile ember carried in the wind,

Daring to burn against the cold.

We laugh,

Even as shadows lengthen,

Our voices defiant, like sparks in the night.

We love,

With hearts unarmoured,

Unafraid of the wounds left by tenderness.

We listen,

To the whispers of the wild,

To the wisdom hidden in the roar of beasts.

We cry,

As rivers carve valleys into the soul,

The weight of the fight pressing heavy on us all.

We wake up,

To the light filtering through battle-torn skies,

A new day born from the ruins.

We sleep,

Dreaming of peace,

Where swords turn to plowshares and lions lie quiet.

We fight,

Because it is written in our blood.

We hope,

Because hope is the only way to survive.

Bring Them Home

At sunset, the sky bleeds shades of orange,

The wind carries whispers of urgency,

Flags flying, their colours vibrant yet heavy,

Each flutter a heartbeat, a cry woven into the air.

Swords of iron glimmer, not with glory,

But with the weight of souls fighting for their lives,

Echoes of history resonate in the distance,

Jews standing firm, a tapestry woven in resilience.

Israel, a land both cradle and crucible,

Hurt lingers like shadows at twilight,

Wounded hearts cling to hope in the dark,

Hostages—where are they? Silent prayers rise,

"Bring them home, bring them home."

Let them feel love, let them feel light,

Illuminate the void with warmth and embrace,

Bring Israel hope, a flame in the night,

So we gather, holding them close,

In a world that spins on the axis of compassion.

Through the turbulence, may we weave threads together,

United in purpose, hands reaching across the divide,

For every soul yearning to return,

May love guide us, as the sun sinks low.

Blue and White

Blue and white, a beacon bright,
The Star of David, our guiding light.
Though hatred rises, fierce and loud,
I stand unshaken, firm, and proud.

A Jew, a Zionist, bold and free,
Israel's heartbeat lives in me.
Its call is strong, it draws me near,
Blue and white, forever dear.

Yet Still, We Rise

Sun waves and sunsets paint the skies,

Israel's beaches where hope never dies.

Alive with life, yet my heart aches,

For those who fall, the toll it takes.

My soul yearns to bring them near,

The hostages we hold so dear.

I hold my breath at every "deal,"

But when it breaks, the pain is real.

Yet still we rise, we will endure,

Our love unyielding, steadfast, pure.

We'll bring them home, each child, each friend,

This broken chapter will find its end.

And on those shores, beneath the blue,

Laughter will echo, dreams renew.

Sun waves and sunsets will shine once more,

On a land united, its people restored.

www.ingramcontent.com/pod-product-compliance
Lightning Source LLC
Chambersburg PA
CBHW072021290426
44109CB00018B/2303